Good Morning and Good Night, Lord:
Daily Prayers for Rise & Rest

Chuck Schlie

DEDICATION & ACKNOWLEDGEMENTS

I dedicate this book to my wife, Mary.

It is with gracious thanks that I give thanks to those who helped in its preparation, especially Stephanie Silbey and Laura Fleetwood.

Proceeds from the sale of this book are given to support Hearts and Hope for Uganda and the annual Night to Shine event at Messiah St. Charles.

Cover designed by Jennifer Ernst.

CONTENTS

FOREWARD

I wrote *Good Morning and Good Night, Lord: Daily Prayers for Rise & Rest* to encourage your life of faith through morning and evening prayer. Here you will find one month's worth of prayers to help you start and end your day. The morning prayers invite God into your life to guide you through the day. The evening prayers reflect on the mercy and grace that He shows you daily. Beginning on Sunday morning and closing on Saturday night, the four weeks of prayers in this book are designed to be prayed over the course of a month and repeated throughout the year.

In 20 years of ministry, I have often been asked how to better incorporate prayer into everyday life. It is my hope that this little book encourages you to speak daily with your Heavenly Father and brings about something good in your life. It will be my joy that your relationship with Him grew closer and your love for His Son Jesus grew stronger as a result of connecting with Him in this way.

In His Name,

Chuck Schlie

WEEK ONE

Sunday Morning

Good morning, Lord God, merciful Father! Thank You for the morning light that wakes me. I pray that You will also wake me up to Light of the Gospel. Open my eyes so that I may see the joy of my salvation and find new strength and hope in You.

Keep me from mindlessly going through the motions as I worship today. Keep me from judging. Keep my mind from wandering. Keep me from just reciting prayers while my heart is far from You. Help me to receive the message of Your Word with excitement. Give me the grace to bring my burdens to the cross and leave them there. May my songs of thankfulness be sung from a very glad heart!

Guide any who have wandered away from the faith back home to You, finding true adventure in the life which is promised to all who follow Jesus. In His name I pray. Amen.

Sunday Night

Good Father in heaven, I pray to You for everything I need, not everything I want. Guide me to finding joy in the little things in this life. Help me to live not for the praise of others but for the humility to obey You.

Savior Jesus, there is no greater opportunity in life than being Your disciple. Thank You for Who You are and all that You have done! Thank You for the possibilities and the joy that comes from loving You, learning from You, and living for You.

Lord Holy Spirit, thank You for the gift of faith. I ask that You would never leave me. You are my Comforter and my Counselor. Lead me where You want me to go this week, and allow me this night to find my rest in You. Good night and Amen.

Monday Morning

Good morning and happy Monday to You, dear Lord! I am so happy to receive the gift of another day in this world! Help me to be a better Christ-follower this week. Give me a big-time faith, a big-time hope, and a big-time love for You and all people.

Keep me from selfishness and pride. Teach me to cast my worries on You. Keep me from the love of money. Watch over me in moments of danger and temptation. Help me to act justly, to love mercy, and to walk humbly with You, my God.

Thank You for all that is coming my way this week. Bless me so that I may be a blessing to others. Let me grab at every chance to do good. Let me be kind and patient and forgiving. Help me to live so beautifully that I would remind someone of Jesus. Grant me the grace to live today as though it were my last on earth and the first with You in heaven. Lord, in Your mercy, hear my prayer. Amen.

Monday Night

God of all comfort, thank You for being so kind to me today. I have sinned against You, but You have not left me. Forgive me and wash me clean.

Grant me a great night of sleep and allow me to rise in the morning, ready to live another day for You. Please watch over my loved ones tonight and keep them safe within Your care.

As I come another day closer to heaven, keep me strong in my faith in Jesus Christ. Direct my thoughts and actions to things eternal so that I don't become too attached to treasures in this life. Give me a sense of balance so that I can be thankful for my earthly blessings without losing interest in my heavenly crown.

Look with mercy upon all who need You: the lonely, the hungry, the hurting, and those without hope. Give me compassion to help them in their need. Make me an extension of Your love. Good night and Amen.

Tuesday Morning

Good morning to You, gracious God! I am so glad that You love me. I am so happy that You like me. I am smiling because You are so very fond of me. I am not worthy of such kindness, but I rejoice in it!

Today, I ask for Your help in living out my calling as Your beloved child. Jesus, if it's a fault for being too kind to a sinner, then it's a fault I learned from You! Help me to do the nicest thing to the rudest person today, because that's Your style. Help me to be gentle. Help me to speak goodness. Help me to live more and more like You.

I am answering Your call to "love one another" as You have loved me. Here I am, Lord, send me on Your mission of love! Amen.

Tuesday Night

You have blessed me again, dear Lord. You have given me more than I could ever ask for or imagine. Accept my heartfelt thanks for Your loving care and mercy.

Bless Your children everywhere. Comfort all who are lonely and in need of love. Help all who are struggling with life. Free us all from the anxieties that plague us. Lift us up from despair. Help us turn to You at all times.

I know You to be good, Lord. Increase my faith in Your loving kindness and in Your almighty power so that I may overcome any fear or trouble and meet tomorrow with confidence. Make me trusting and calm. Keep me close to You. I am Yours. Good night and Amen.

Wednesday Morning

Good morning! It is with a grateful heart I rise to praise You, O Lord, for You have refreshed me with a restful sleep and have graciously given me another new day. You have made this day and it belongs to You.

I ask that every word that comes from my mouth tells of Your presence in my life. Make me thoughtful, patient, and considerate at work. Remove from my heart all bitterness and resentment and help me smile at the unpleasant situations that I am sure to encounter this side of heaven.

Protect me from temptation, from doubt and worry, from cold-heartedness and carelessness. Keep me from being so busy that I become frazzled instead of fearless. Don't let me get caught up in the trap of feeling sorry for myself. You have set me free, Lord. Help me to enjoy the freedom to love and to be loved. I go into this day happily with You by my side. Amen.

Wednesday Night

Come to me, Lord Jesus. Walk across the water and bring my heart the knowledge of full forgiveness and Your peace which passes all understanding. Relax my body and give me much-needed rest. Remove all worries from my mind and let me sleep comfortably as You watch over me.

Bless Your people far and near and give healing and strength to the sick. If I have made someone sad or angry today, forgive me. If I have sinned against You today, forgive me. If I have been thoughtless and unkind, forgive me. Guide me to be less sinful tomorrow.

Protect me and my loved ones from worry and doubt. Keep Your followers from bitterness and selfishness. Keep us in the faith. Keep us humble and pure in heart. Hear my prayer, dear Savior and Friend. Good night and Amen.

Thursday Morning

Good morning! At the beginning of another day, Father in heaven, it is good to know You are with me. Help me to remember that being happy doesn't mean that I have it all but that I'm thankful for all that I have. You have given me so much!

I don't know what is in store for me today, but I trust that You will give me all that I need to handle whatever good or bad this day may bring. I trust Your promise that You will make every experience work together for my good.

I am thankful for the opportunities that this day offers to provide me with what I need. Use all circumstances to teach me Your values and may they be revealed in all that I think and say and do. Keep me faithful to Jesus. I'd rather be rejected by people for being a follower of Christ than to have to explain to You why I rejected Him in front of others.

I don't want anything from You Lord but Your presence and guidance in my life. Amen.

Thursday Night

Dear Father, I know that You don't love me because of whatever good I manage to do. You love me because You just do. What a relief! I am so thankful that You have forgiven me for my many sins. I have the wonderful assurance that I am Your child and You are my Heavenly Father — and Jesus Christ is my Savior and Friend!

I am so thankful that You are not done with me. You are writing my story, and I apologize for the times that I try to take the pen from Your hand. Remind me throughout the day that You are the Author, and I am just a little pencil. Write Your love to the world through me. I do not ask for something big or amazing or spectacular; just something ordinary but good.

Help me to love my family. Help me to love my neighbors. Help me to love those I work with. Help me to love the stranger, the broken, and the hurting. Help me especially to love someone far from You. Help me even to love me.

I love You. Good night and Amen.

Friday Morning

Good morning, Jesus! You pulled off Your own death and resurrection. For this I rejoice in Your awesome power and glory! I ask that You keep me from temptation today. I know that Satan prowls all around and is looking to take me down the wrong road.

Dear Lord, You know my sinful heart and how it so easily wanders from You. Give me the grace to recognize temptation when it comes. Fill my heart with Your Holy Spirit so that I may overcome it in Your great name.

Help me be the reason that someone knows You. Be in me and with me so others will know that You are good. Help me to be the person who can make everybody feel like a somebody. Help me to be a nobody, trying to tell everybody about You, the Somebody who saved my soul.

I am looking forward to the adventure of this day with You. Amen.

Friday Night

Merciful Father, thank You for work and thank You for rest. Your goodness has given me even more than I need. And You have done more – so much more! Your heart has drawn me closer to You. Truly, You are wonderful and worthy of praise!

Make me thankful every day and night for Your many blessings. Let me count them one by one with a grateful heart: this morning I woke and I could walk; I opened my eyes and I could see; I reached for my food and I could enjoy it. Your provisions have no limit!

How often I have forgotten to thank You for peace of mind, for the erasure of my sin, for the very air I breathe, and for the water I drink. The beauty of the world which You have made is truly astonishing. Lord, make me truly appreciate all of it.

Above all, thank You for giving me a Savior who loves me and walks with me. In Your grace, lull me to sleep with a thankful heart. Good night and Amen.

Saturday Morning

Good morning, Lord Jesus, the Sun of all that is right! Shine into my heart and life today. Help me reflect Your light on someone who needs You.

Thank You for taking away all that is wrong about me and placing it upon Yourself. You died for my transgressions and have erased all my past, present, and future sins. You have deposited into my spiritual account all that is good with You.

Saturday is a day off of my vocational work, and I'm thankful for the rest. Remind me that every day is an opportunity to be "on" for You. Help me give my best to You by giving my best to others today. Keep me united with You so that I may draw on Your strength to love others. I want to do Your good work today. If I succeed, I want You to get all the credit and all of the glory, for it truly is Yours! I do it for love. Amen.

Saturday Night

Lord Jesus, You have come that I may have life and have it to the full. I praise You with all my heart for the enjoyment I have received from Your goodness and love. Your continual presence has made the day brighter. Even though I have stumbled and failed, You have not turned away from me. If I did anything good, I'm thankful for it because it came by Your Spirit.

Bless me this night with a peaceful and refreshing sleep so that I may be fully present to worship You tomorrow. Inspire the preaching of Your Word so that what I hear gets into my heart. I don't want to sleepwalk through worship. I have every reason to sing Your praises. You are the Hope of the world. You are my hope too!

Teach me Your ways, O Lord. Students learn best from teachers they love, and I love You. Good night, dear Teacher, dear Savior, dear Redeemer. Good night, my dearest Friend. Amen.

WEEK TWO

Sunday Morning

Good morning, Heavenly Father. Holy is Your name! Help me this day to come into Your presence with great thankfulness in my heart as I join with others to worship You. Give me joy as I worship my Savior, knowing that He has done it all!

Fill my pastor with Your grace and truth. Lead him to speak Your Word courageously and convincingly, so that the hearts of all who hear may come closer to You. Send Your Holy Spirit into the hearts of people everywhere so that they may believe and be saved.

Help all of us know the good You want for us and the ability to carry it out. By Your Spirit make me pure in heart and mind. May all that I do please You this day. In Jesus' name I request this help. Amen.

Sunday Night

Gracious God, thank You for the blessings of this day. I am so thankful for the forgiveness of my sins and the new life and salvation that I have in You.

Lord God, Heavenly Father, watch over me tonight. Strengthen me for tomorrow so that I may serve You and the people around me with a smile on my face.

Lord Jesus Christ, make me grateful for Your life, Your death, and Your resurrection. You are my Good Shepherd. Take me by the hand and lead me for all of my days.

Lord God Holy Spirit, keep me in the saving faith. Increase my love and trust that I may walk humbly and serve God with all of my heart, mind, soul, and strength.

I ask for a great night's sleep and joy in my heart as I wake in the morning. Good night and Amen.

Monday Morning

Good morning, Heavenly Father! Your kingdom come and Your will be done today! Take control of this world. Rule it! Hold back the wicked and give the countries of this world honest and peaceful governments so harmony may abound everywhere.

Rule Your church, Lord! Bless the teaching of Your Word so that many more people may come to know You. Bless all who are followers of Your Son and strengthen their faith so they may be salt and light in the world today.

Rule my heart, Lord, and help me grow in the knowledge of Your love. Bless my work today. Make me do something wonderful that points someone to Jesus.

Rule the hearts and lives of everyone I love. Watch over my family and friends. Keep us all close to You. In the name of Jesus, may Your will be done. Amen.

Monday Night

Lord, I thank You for the blessings which You have freely given me on this first workday of the week: for safety as I went to and from work; for health and strength to be useful; for the food and clothes and shelter that was bought as a result of my work. Thank You for employment!

Help me to keep improving at my work. Help me to remember that I am not just serving myself but also You and all those around me. Make me always willing to do my very best at my job. Give me a peaceful heart when things don't go my way. Help me to honor those I work for and to love those I work with, remembering always Your own great love for me and all people.

As I fall asleep, give me joy in my Savior Jesus Christ and full trust in Him that I have everything I need – the forgiveness of sins and the certainty of eternal life. Good night and Amen.

Tuesday Morning

Good morning, Lord! You are good and kind and altogether wonderful! I have peace in You! I have joy in You! I have hope in You! Thank You, Lord, for this good life and forgive me when I do not love it enough.

Look on me today with Your blessing and help me through the difficult times in my life. Be with me as I encounter disappointments, hardships, and struggles. Keep me from the temptation to be lazy and cynical. Guard my heart against all worry and doubt. Graciously take me by the hand and lead me into each hour of the day.

I lift up to You all who are weary and burdened, all who are discouraged, all who mourn and weep, and all who are lonely and afraid. Draw them closer to You. Draw any of them closer to me so that I may be of some good to them. Keep my eyes open. Keep my heart open. Keep me with You, Jesus, my Savior and sweetest Friend. Amen.

Tuesday Night

Lord God, my Father in Christ Jesus, I don't know what tomorrow will bring, but because I have You I am not afraid. You have promised to never leave me, and that is all the knowledge I need. I place myself in Your care tonight, certain that You will be with me tomorrow.

Save me from the trappings of sin. Keep my heart free of envy, bitterness, resentment, and arrogance. Bless me with the great gifts of the Fruit of the Spirit: love, joy, peace, patience, kindness, goodness, faithfulness, gentleness, and self-control.

May all that I do and say give honor and praise to Your Son Jesus Christ, my Savior. As You are with me with tonight, let me be Yours forever. Good night and Amen.

Wednesday Morning

Good morning to You, O God Eternal. Thank You for opening my eyes to see another day of life full of Your promises and blessings. May I accept each and every one with a thankful heart. Help me not to let the troubles of this day rob me of any cheerful outlook on life that is mine because of the faith that I have in Jesus Christ my Lord.

If I become discouraged today, let me come to You and lean against You in prayer. Abide with me. Isn't that a wonderful word, Lord? *Abide.* Abide with me, and I will abide with You. Keep me in Your grace and let this day be one that is rich in life and service to You and all people.

Direct my heart and mouth to praise You throughout the day. Amen.

Wednesday Night

As the day comes to a close, I worship You, my God. My grateful heart is filled with love for You. I know You. I know that Your loving kindness has blessed me and that Your guidance has protected me this day. In Your goodness You have opened Your hand and have given me more than I needed. You have encouraged me and forgiven me all my sins. Truly, You are wonderful, O Lord.

Bless me and those I love with a great night of sleep. Let my soul have peace and my heart, body, and mind have rest with You. In the name of Jesus, good night and Amen.

Thursday Morning

This is the day that You have made, so I will rejoice and be glad in it! Good morning, Lord. Thank You for watching over me last night and for the gift of another day to live for You.

Keep me dependent on You for every little thing today. Help me see that every good and perfect gift is from You, for You are my Father and I am Your child.

In my heart, I am not strong enough to really ask for it, but You know best; and so I pray that if You need to, send me trials and disappointments so that I may be humbled to know that I am not God. If trouble comes to me, let me turn to You. Keep Your eyes on me, O Lord, and my eyes always on You.

Let this day be a day of happiness with You. Let this day be a day of joy in You. Let this day be a day of love for You. Amen.

Thursday Night

Heavenly Father, Your mercies were new this morning, and they did not fail me. Thank You for being so faithful and kind and generous to me this day. I do not deserve that kind of love, for I did not love You or love my neighbors the way I should have today. Forgive me for my unkind words, impure thoughts, and selfish actions.

There are sins that I know and regret. If I have unknowingly hurt anyone today, please forgive me. If I have neglected an opportunity to do good today, please forgive me. If I have loved the world a little too much and You a little too little, please forgive me. Do not take Your Holy Spirit from me, but restore to me the joy of my salvation.

Surround me with Your protection and loving care. Remove all my fears and scatter all doubts from my heart. Keep me strong in my faith. Good night and Amen.

Friday Morning

Good morning, Heavenly Father! Thank You for last night's rest and for the opportunities which this new day brings. May I serve You faithfully. As I go about my daily tasks, help me to be kind to those with whom I come into contact.

Remind me that all people matter and that You dearly love them. Press upon my heart that You want all people to be saved and come to know You through Your Son.

When things go wrong today, do not let me sulk. Rather, remind me to look to You for help. Teach me not to dwell on earthly matters and instead put my focus on heavenly values. I don't want anything more than the honor of being called Your child. Stay close by me and watch over those I love. I ask this in the name of my Savior Jesus, Who shed His blood for me. Amen.

Friday Night

Gracious God, stay with me. I praise and thank You. Your goodness and mercy have protected me again today and have brought me safely home. Whatever I have done wrong, forgive me, dear Lord. If I have failed to love all others, or if I have disobeyed Your Word, for Jesus' sake take my sins as far away as the east is from the west.

Let Your care surround me and Your children everywhere. Bless all who seek to do Your good work. Protect all who serve our country. Grant wisdom to all who are in authority. Your kingdom come. Your will be done, in my life and throughout the world. Grant this, dear Lord, for Jesus' sake. Good night and Amen.

Saturday Morning

Good morning, dear Father in heaven. Deliver me from evil. I know that my Savior has promised that no one can snatch me from His hand. Yet, I am prone to wander. Give me the grace that I may not sin and bring evil on myself. When troubles arise, use them to strengthen me and draw me closer to Your heart.

I pray for Your blessings and a grateful heart with which to receive them. Help me to be content. Help me to enjoy the day. May my words be grace-filled and Your Spirit lead my actions. Help me use the resources and talents that You have given me to bless people today.

Ultimately, I ask that You do what is best for me today. I know that You work the good in all things for those who love You and are called according to Your purpose. I believe it. Amen.

Saturday Night

Lord, I thank You that You have given me health and strength to finish another week of earthly life. I really am thankful for it. Thank You for the blessings of my work, my family, and my friendships. Thank You for Your care and protection, Your Word and Your power, Your love and Your forgiveness. Help me daily to remember that all these blessings are a gift from You and that without You I would be absolutely miserable.

Keep my community and my country in peace. Guard Your church against the Evil One. Bless all teachers and the students in their care. Comfort the sorrowful, provide for the poor, and use me to do Your good. Let the things that break Your heart break my own and then put me to loving, good work on Your behalf.

Protect me tonight. Give me refreshing sleep so I may worship You with all my heart in the morning. Good night and Amen

Week 2

WEEK THREE

Sunday Morning

Good morning, dear Savior! I have every reason in the world to worship You for You have saved me from my sins and blessed me with Your love and mercy. You have been so kind to me.

Bless the preaching of Your Word throughout the world today so that many people of every nation may be brought to faith in You. Bless my hearing of Your Word today that I may be strengthened in my faith and have the desire to serve You all the more. Keep me aware that I must not be just a listener of Your Word, but a doer of what pleases You. Help me to live out the grace and mercy You so generously give me.

All praise, glory, and honor are Yours, dear Jesus! Amen.

Sunday Night

Heavenly Father, I want to thank You for this day. Thank You for every little thing. I pray that the blessings of this day, especially the hearing of Your Word, the singing of Your praises, and the feeling of Your presence would go with me throughout the upcoming week.

I praise You most of all for Your mercy and grace in Jesus Christ. You did not have to, but You have drawn me closer to You with loving kindness. I could never repay You for all that You have done for me. All I have is my thankfulness and the dedication of my life.

For this night, I give myself over to You. Let Your holy angels be with me. I am in Your hands. Good night and Amen.

Monday Morning

Good morning, Heavenly Father! Thank You for having kept me safe during the night. Let me pause at the beginning of another week of work to ask You to go with me. I do not know what this week will bring – good or bad, health or sickness, sunshine or shadow. However, since You go with me, I am not afraid. I rely on Your presence every step of the way. On this Monday morning I pray that You will stay close beside me. Though I do not know what the future holds, I know Who holds the future.

Bless me in whatever I do. Make me strong physically, mentally, morally, and spiritually. Watch over me and over those I love. I ask this in the name of Your Son, my Savior and Redeemer. Amen.

Monday Night

Thank You, dear Heavenly Father who created day and night, for the care that You have given me today. I do not deserve the many blessings that come from Your hand, but I am so thankful for them. I ask that You forgive my sins of the day, especially if I have offended someone who is not connected to Jesus. Forgive me if I missed an opportunity to lead someone to You. Help me to grow in Your Spirit's power so that each day my faith may be built up more and more and more.

Guard my home and protect those who live with me under this roof that You have provided us. Bless the friends I love. Look with mercy upon all people. Comfort those who have experienced sadness. Have the Good News of Jesus' love reach the hearts of all people. Give to me and all others a greater appreciation of Your mercy so that we may serve You more joyfully tomorrow. Be with me always. Good night and Amen.

Tuesday Morning

Good morning, my Heavenly Father! At the beginning of this new day I ask You for the gift of Your Holy Spirit and the gift of a new spirit within me. As You have kept me safe throughout the night, continue to watch over me and keep me from all that is wrong for me to do or say.

Open my eyes for every chance to do something good. Give me faithfulness for every job that is set before me. Grant me the grace to serve all people as I would serve You.

Help me live this day as if Jesus died yesterday, arose today, and were coming back tomorrow. May I have enough success today to be encouraged and enough difficulties to be humbled. Give me the strength to not give in to do what is wrong and to seize my opportunities to do good. Amen.

Tuesday Night

Lord Jesus, You welcome all who come to You and so I come. I come burdened with my sins and I ask You to forgive me once again. I have not done today all that You have asked me to do. I know that I am a sinner but all the more I know that You came for sinners; therefore, I ask that You remember my sins no more.

Help me to be stronger because of Your forgiveness, happier because of Your mercy, and more willing to serve You and others because of Your love.

You have been my Refuge and Strength, my ever-present Help in trouble. You have been my Shield and my Reward. How can I thank You enough for Your kindness, and how can I stop praising Your beautiful name?

I give my body and soul to Your safekeeping. You are faithful, and I trust in You. Good night and Amen.

Wednesday Morning

Good morning! To You, O Lord, do I lift up my heart this day, sincerely happy for another shot at life! Bless me in what I do today. I want to put a smile on Your face! I ask for just enough success as You deem best for me. Let me always remember that everything in life depends on Your great grace and blessing.

Help me, I pray, to have the love of my Savior Jesus Christ spill over into the lives of others. In all my dealings with other people guide me to love them as I love myself, and to do for them what You have done for me.

Strengthen me to stand up to any temptation. Give me the courage to suffer a loss rather than inflict trouble on others. Remind me not to collect the trappings of the world and instead strive for the things that money cannot buy. Help me to be content with what You have blessed me with. Teach me to know that my true treasure is in heaven. In Jesus' name I pray, and in His name I begin my day. Amen.

Wednesday Night

Heavenly Father, thank You for the honor of speaking to You in prayer. How good it is to know that I can come to You and whisper in Your ear. It is even more wonderful that You invite me to do so and that You want to hear from me! Give me the faith of a loving child, never doubting that You love me and listen to me. If sometimes You do not answer my prayers exactly as I have asked, then let me have the child-like trust to believe that You know what is best for me.

Father, I ask that You take into Your special care all those who are burdened with the worries and troubles of this world. Watch over all who are sick. Comfort those who are living with the loss of a loved one. Reveal Yourself to them as their Heavenly Father whom they may turn to in any time of trouble.

And now, let me find peace and a refreshing night of sleep. Good night and Amen.

Thursday Morning

Good morning, dear Heavenly Father. Thank You for the gift of forgiveness! I need this assurance of Your mercy today as I am going to sin and others will sin against me. I wish this weren't true, but I know better. So in advance, I ask that You please forgive me my sins and help me – in thankfulness to You – to forgive those who sin against me.

Lord, I know that down deep I am proud and think too highly of myself. I too easily overlook my wrong-doing. Help me see who I really am without Your mercy – a lost and condemned sinner. God, be merciful to me!

Make me aware of my struggles to be obedient to You and remind me that others have similar struggles. When someone sins against me, help me to be kind to them as You have been kind to me. Give me an understanding heart, a forgiving heart, and a loving heart. When I sin against someone, please help them to forgive me so that together we may walk in the way of life, for Jesus' sake. Amen.

Thursday Night

Lord and Savior Jesus Christ, tonight I bring before You the needs of my church. I thank You for my pastor and for all who teach the Gospel near and far.

Lord, it seems that Your church isn't loved like it should be. But You love it. You created it. You died for it. Help me and all who belong to Your church exalt You in our actions. Help us to have joy as we spread Your Gospel. Help us learn from Your Word and put it into practice. Help us through our words and actions demonstrate Your great love for sinners. Make us (make *me*) excited to share this Good News! Give me an opportunity to tell of Your glory and the grace to speak Your Word when I have the chance to witness for You.

Help me to share Your love with my family, my friends, and especially with those who don't know You as their Savior. And now, I ask for a peaceful rest. Renew my body and spirit for tomorrow. Good night and Amen.

Friday Morning

Good morning, dear Savior Jesus Christ! I praise You for saving my life through Your good work on the cross and Your resurrection from the grave! You have bought me and I am all Yours. Today I want to serve You with a willing heart to show my appreciation for all that You have done for me. Make me an instrument of Your peace.

With Your Spirit and Your strength, help me reveal You to others today. By Your grace help me resist every temptation to sin. Do what You will in me so that I do some good. Help me to never be ashamed to be called a "Christ-follower." I pray for a genuine joy in and sincere thankfulness of Your goodness.

When an encouraging word is needed, let me give it. When a helping hand is needed, make mine ready. Guide my footsteps in ways that are pleasing to You and a blessing to those I will cross paths with today. May my whole day be dedicated to You, my Savior and Friend. Let's go! Amen.

Friday Night

Lord, with a grateful heart I come into Your presence tonight, keeping in my mind all the blessings You have given me throughout this day. You have forgiven my sins, comforted me in my disappointments, calmed me when I was upset, and strengthened me in the face of temptations and doubt.

I love You, Lord of heaven and earth, for Your goodness and kindness to me. May I always be as faithful to You as You have been to me. Draw me closer to You. Bring to my heart that peace that Jesus won for me. Remove all worry and fear from me this night so that I may sleep knowing that all is well because You are with me. When morning comes, let Your presence guide me through the day, Your goodness always present in my mind. Good night and Amen.

Saturday Morning

Good morning, Father in heaven. I come to You this morning thankful for this day! Thank You for my eyes to see, ears to hear, and mouth to speak. Thank You for creating me and my family and my friends. Thank You for food to eat and a roof over my head. Thank You for my soft bed, warm water in the shower, and everything indoors. Thank You for the sun, the sky, plants, animals, and everything outdoors. You are so inventive!

Good morning, Jesus my Savior! I come to You today in thankfulness for coming to save me from my sins. I thank You for Your good work on the cross and Your resurrection from the grave. I thank You for how strong You are. I thank You for how gentle You are. I thank You for You!

Good morning, Holy Spirit! The entire created world is Your playground. Draw me into Your play. I want to live with You because in You I find relationship with my Father and true life in Christ! Keep me close to You as I live and move and play and rest! Thank You, Amen.

Saturday Night

My gracious God, at the end of another week I thank You that You have kept me from all danger of body and soul. I am grateful, too, that You have blessed me with the work that I do. I am not worthy to receive any of Your goodness and mercy…but I am so thankful for it! Continue to bless me with whatever is for my ultimate good.

In the quietness of this hour, I ask that You prepare my heart to worship You tomorrow. Bless the preaching of Your Word throughout the world so that You may bring many closer and closer to Jesus.

I ask that You send Your Holy Spirit to my church tomorrow. May the hearing of the Gospel strengthen our faith in You, the One true God revealed as Father, Son, and Holy Spirit.

With the knowledge that You, Heavenly Father, truly do love me, I rest and delight. I am in Your good hands. Good night and Amen.

WEEK FOUR

Sunday Morning

Good morning, loving Father! Make Your love come alive to me as I worship You today. Let Your Holy Spirit have free reign in my heart so that my faith grows stronger and my commitment to serve You increases. May nothing be more precious to me than the Good News of Jesus who saved me from my sins!

Create in me a clean heart, a fresh heart, a new heart. Remove all distracting thoughts as I come into Your presence to hear Your Word and offer my prayers. I also ask that You would surprise me in a good way today. Wake me up so I don't go through the motions. Fill my heart with peace and joy and forgiveness.

Do what You want in me. Let Your love conquer my doubts and fears and my selfish moods. On this day of worship, let me sing my praises to You – and really mean it. Help me to dedicate myself again to Your Son Jesus Christ, who is worthy of all worship, glory, honor, and praise. Amen.

Sunday Night

As this day comes to a close, I thank You for Your goodness and mercy. Your promises help me look forward to the future with courage. I pray for Your continued blessings as I head into Monday morning. Make Your presence in my life known.

Deepen my love for You. Keep me faithful to You. Bless me this night, and protect all Your children. Bless my family and my friends. Bless those who serve my community as law enforcement officers, fire-fighters, and rescue workers. Bless my president, governor, and mayor. Bless those who serve in the military. Bless all doctors and nurses. Bless pastors and teachers. Bless those who are hungry, lonely, and imprisoned. Bless my enemies too. In Jesus' name I ask this. Good night and Amen.

Monday Morning

Good morning, my Lord and my God! You have called me by my name and I am Yours. Thank You for having loved me with a love that goes on forever. I know that there is nothing that I can do wrong that would make You love me any less. I know that there is nothing I could do right that would make You love me even more. Thank You for Your perfect love for me.

This morning I pray that You would give me the determination to live like Jesus. Help me to live out my thankfulness by being cheerful and trusting. Help me to be what You want me to be, and when I fail, forgive me. Let Your grace strengthen my desire to love You and all people.

You have called me out of darkness and into Your wonderful light. Give me the joy of living as a child of light and a citizen of heaven, so that others may be drawn to You and to Jesus, who is the Light of the world. Amen.

Monday Night

God of love and grace, tonight I ask You to forgive me for all that I did wrong today. I admit that at times I find myself doing what I don't want to do, and other times I do not do what I know I should do. Have mercy on me! Send Your Holy Spirit to me so that I may grow in grace and in knowledge of my Savior, Jesus Christ. Help me to be full of everything that is pleasing to You.

I pray for all who are down because of sickness or loss, and I ask that You apply healing to their wounded hearts.

Let this night be a peaceful one, so that I may get after loving You and loving others tomorrow. Good night and Amen.

Tuesday Morning

Good morning, Heavenly Father! Let Your will be done on earth as it is in heaven. I pray that Your will be done in the hearts and lives of people everywhere. Help me today and always to be aware of Your will for my life. Give me faithfulness in my work today and to my friends and family always.

Keep me and all Christians mindful of Your commandments and give us the ability to live them out. Above all, give us a burning love for people and a sense of urgency to tell of the great love of Jesus Christ to any who are not yet in a saving relationship with Him.

May I trust Your Word and ask of You nothing more than what You have promised me. Keep me humble during the good times and keep me strong in the middle of tough times. At all times, give me a deep love for You. In Jesus' name, Amen.

Tuesday Night

Dear Father in heaven, thank You for answering my prayers and the prayers of Your children everywhere. Be with me tonight and keep all danger from me. Forgive my sins and quiet me with Your love. Keep all who are dear to me close to Your heart.

Cleanse my heart from all thoughts of anger or envy. Help me to live joyfully and contentedly. Make me helpful, kind, and considerate so that I may live my life for You and for others.

May thoughts of Your goodness fill my heart when I fall asleep and when I awake. I rest in You. Good night and Amen.

Wednesday Morning

Good morning, Lord Jesus! You are my ever-living and ever-loving Savior! Thank you for having kept watch over me throughout the night, and I pray that You would open my eyes to see the blessings You have prepared for me today. For the love of friends which will bring me joy, I thank You. For the ability to work and provide for myself and others, I praise You. For all of the gifts You give, I honor You.

Keep me strong in the faith, watchful when tempted to do wrong, humble in success, and cheerful in the face of trouble. Without You, I can do nothing. But through You and the strength You give me, I can do all things!

Help me to be clear today about who is the Boss of me and the Lord of my life. Use me to bring the Gospel to someone who is like a lost sheep without a shepherd, so that they too may know You as the Good Shepherd and find peace and rest for their soul in Your care. Lead me in paths of righteousness for Your name's sake. I thank You that my cup overflows. Amen.

Wednesday Night

At the end of another day, dear Heavenly Father, I praise You for Your goodness and I love You for Your mercy. There is nothing better than being close to You. I thank You for every breath, for every heartbeat, for every act of sight and hearing, for every second of every day – I thank You!

From the rising of the sun to the shadows of the night, You have been with me and for me. You have helped me and guided me and strengthened me and protected me and have comforted me. For all these provisions I thank You!

Lord, You have many weak children in Your family, many dull students in Your school, and many lame sheep in Your flock. I know this too well, because I am one of them. Yet, You never leave me. You love me. You cherish me. You think I'm great. Your grace really is amazing! Help me to freely give Your kind of grace away tomorrow. Good night and Amen.

Thursday Morning

Good morning, gracious Father in heaven! Today I ask for humility. I don't want to be anyone special. I don't need to feel important. I don't desire fame, reward, or praise. I don't require promotion, popularity, or intelligence. I don't have to win arguments. I don't need to show off so people think I'm a somebody. Please help me, because I often forget that You place no value on such pursuits. Help me to be the person You desire me to be.

I want to be Your fully engaged disciple. I want to love people. I want to give my best. I want to sacrifice. I want to be strong in my faith. I want to trust more, hope more, and love more.

I thank You that my past is forgiven and that my future is secure. I don't know what day You will call me home, but I know that the road of my life leads ultimately to Your loving arms. In the meantime, lead me and I will gladly follow. Guide me here on earth until I reach my heavenly home. In Jesus' name. Amen.

Thursday Night

As this day is ending, dear Heavenly Father, I come to You to thank You for Your unfailing love. The wrongs and mistakes that I have made today show me again how much I need Your grace. Forgive me for Jesus' sake, and take away every impure thought and wish. Make my heart right and make my actions reflect Your love. I want to be more like Jesus, who went around doing good. I want to be more loving and more forgiving. Help me, O Lord.

Heal the sick, relieve the hurting, strengthen the weak, bring home the wandering, calm the anxious, restrain the wicked, help the troubled, rescue the lost, comfort the broken-hearted, and give peace to the dying.

O Lord who does not sleep, keep me safe until morning comes again. Good night and Amen.

Friday Morning

Good morning, Almighty God, Heavenly Father! Thank you for the talents You have given me. Help me to make the best possible use of them today. In all that I do, give me the guidance to choose that which is good and run away from sin before I get caught up in it.

Father, I ask that You send me someone who needs to be loved today. Send me someone who needs encouragement. Send me someone who needs to know that they matter. Send me someone who could use a smile. Send me someone who could use a hug. Maybe even send me someone who needs my lunch. Help me to remember that whatever I do for the least of humanity, I do for Jesus.

Let's pull off a kindness caper today! It will be our secret adventure. If I fail on my end, forgive me and give me another chance tomorrow. If I happen to succeed, then all thanks to You for having done it through me. I'm looking forward to what You have in store! I go with You. Amen.

Friday Night

My Father in heaven, it is really a mind-blower to think about Your love for me. When I consider that Your hand made me and created me to be the person that I am, I am at a loss for words. I'm not bragging on me, I'm bragging on You. Thank You for making me one-of-a-kind and allowing me to have life and – through Jesus – to have it to the full!

I admit that I don't live up to all that You want for me and ask of me. Help me to make the most of what You have given me. Help me to be myself, a feat I too often find challenging. Teach me not to be jealous of others. Too often I try to be someone else, to imitate others, forgetting that You made me to be *me*.

Help me understand myself. Reveal to me the unique gifts You have blessed me with to do Your work here on earth. Help me to see who I am and what I can do. Give me the courage to love and serve You in the ways You have equipped me. Above all, grow my faith and trust in You that I may always remain Your child. Good night and Amen.

Saturday Morning

Good morning, dear Lord! Thank You for Saturday! As I begin a new day with You, search my heart and remove anything that does not please You. Help me to put You first in everything.

Help me to overcome the temptations I will face today. Guard my thoughts and especially help me keep my big mouth in check. Keep me from griping and complaining. Help me build others up and keep me from cutting anyone down. I need Your great help in having me put the best construction on everything.

Have me stop throughout the day to give You my thanks. Thank You for all the blessings of the past. Thank You for the enjoyment of this day. Thank You for the future plans, especially the eternal plans that You have for me, all because of Jesus Christ my Savior. In His name I pray. Amen.

Saturday Night

Gracious Father, as I look back on the day, I have every reason to be thankful. You have made me Your own, forgiven my sins, and have kept me in the faith. I lift my heart and voice in praise to You and ask You to continue to be with me tonight.

Bless our home, our church, and our nation. Give our missionaries great courage to boldly proclaim Your love and truth to all people. I look forward to the privilege of worshiping my Savior tomorrow. Grant me the grace to believe what I will hear from Your Word, and give me the joy that comes from giving You my praise.

Lord, You have opened my eyes to the beauty of Your love. Now, I ask that You close my eyes in rest and let me see the morning sunshine of Your kindness and the brightness of the true life I have in You. Good night and Amen.

ADDITIONAL
PRAYERS

Morning

Good morning, Gracious God! Thank You for giving me a brand new day! Help me to face it with joy and a smile no matter what happens. May everything I do bring You happiness! No matter how big a challenge I encounter is, help me face it with confidence. No matter how small the opportunity to do good is, let me grab it.

Give me the spirit and the energy to carry out the calling You have set before me. As I go about my day, give me an attitude that reveals the difference it makes in my life to know You! In Jesus' name I pray. Amen.

Night

My Father, I woke up this morning not knowing for sure what this day would bring. But You knew, and now, You have brought me to this night. Thank You for this day and all the opportunities You gave me to honor You and bless others. Thank You for all who blessed me.

Lord, I know that You are with me and that I am never alone, but I pray for those who don't know You and have not experienced Your presence. I ask for Your love to fill the lives of those who need You most. Surround them with people who can be the hands and feet and voice of Jesus. Could You make me one of those people?

Bless me with a night of rest and send me out with joy into Your harvest fields tomorrow. Good night and Amen.

Morning

Good morning, dear Lord! I would like to be a person of thanksgiving today! Help me to smile throughout this day in deep appreciation for everything. I want to see the beauty in nature. I want to see the beauty in people. I want to look at all that You have made and be glad.

Help me to see hardships as an opportunity to trust You. Give me eyes to see how You are working in my life. I want to stop comparing myself with others and be grateful for how You made me. I bet that You want those things for me too!

Give me the grace to be a thankful child. Only Your Holy Spirit can give me a heart of praise, and so I ask for that today. Amen.

Night

Dear Heavenly Father, thank You for Your ongoing mercy and for all of the blessings You have showered upon me today. Everything is a gift from You! This is the day that You have made. Thank You for all I was able to accomplish today. Thank You for the memories that have been made. Thank You for keeping me in Your care. Yes, through it all, You have been by my side.

Forgive all that was wrong in me this day. Help me to forgive those who have wronged me.

Please give to me and all whom I love a restful night of sleep so that we may wake up in the morning renewed and ready to serve You. In our Savior's name I pray. Good night and Amen.

Morning

Good morning, my Heavenly Father! Thank You for keeping me safe throughout the night. I pray that You would keep me safe throughout this new day. Keep me from sinning and may all that I do today please You.

I ask for an inward happiness and the peace that comes from living close to You. How wonderful it is to know that You are with me on the path before me today. Help me to see that even what is ordinary can be gifts from You, something You've prepared just for me to experience. Help me to also recognize the unusual and unexpected delights You put in my path.

Grant that I never pass by someone You put in my way today without showing them the love of Jesus Christ. In His name I pray. Amen.

Night

Lord and Savior, I come to You filled with sadness over the fact that You had to die to save me. I also come to You filled with happiness over the fact that You did so willingly. I come before You tonight with a debt that I could never repay but the full knowledge that You have freed me from that debt. Your grace allows me to stand with You in complete forgiveness and joy! Truly, You are wonderful, O Lord!

Thank You for all You did to make everything right. You reconciled me to God. Thank You for never giving up on me. I am so grateful that You love me so deeply. I am so thankful to be Yours forever. You are mine, my dearest Friend. Good night and Amen.

Made in USA - Crawfordsville, IN
25953_9798580093284
06.16.2022 2229